United States Government Accountability Office

Report to the Chairman, Subcommittee on Social Security, Committee on Ways and Means, House of Representatives

June 2014

RAILROAD RETIREMENT BOARD

Total and Permanent Disability Program at Risk of Improper Payments

RAILROAD RETIREMENT BOARD

Total and Permanent Disability Program at Risk of Improper Payments

GAO Highlights

Highlights of GAO-14-418, a report to the Chairman, Subcommittee on Social Security, Committee on Ways and Means, House of Representatives

Why GAO Did This Study

In recent years, the U.S. Department of Justice has investigated and prosecuted railroad workers who were suspected of falsely claiming over $1 billion in disability benefits, raising concerns about RRB's disability claims process. GAO was asked to evaluate the integrity of RRB's disability program. This report examines (1) whether RRB's policies and procedures for processing claims were adequate to ensure that only eligible claimants receive T&P disability benefits; and (2) the extent to which RRB's management strategy ensures that approved claims are accurate and addresses program risks. To answer these questions, GAO reviewed T&P determination policies and procedures, interviewed RRB officials in headquarters and four district offices—selected for geographic dispersion—reviewed relevant federal laws and regulations, and reviewed a nongeneralizable random sample of 10 T&P cases that were approved in fiscal year 2012 to illustrate RRB's claims process.

What GAO Recommends

GAO recommends that RRB explore options for obtaining more timely earnings information; revise its policy concerning the supervisory review of disability claims; establish a regular quality assurance review of T&P disability decisions; develop a performance goal to track decision accuracy; and develop and implement fraud awareness policies, procedures, and annual training. RRB agreed with these recommendations.

View GAO-14-418. For more information, contact Dan Bertoni at (202) 512-7215 or bertonid@gao.gov.

What GAO Found

The Railroad Retirement Board's (RRB) policies and procedures for processing total and permanent (T&P) disability benefit claims do not adequately ensure that claimants meet program eligibility requirements. To find a railroad worker eligible for T&P benefits, RRB makes an independent determination of disability using the same general criteria that the Social Security Administration (SSA) uses to administer its Disability Insurance (DI) program—that is, a worker must have a medically determinable physical or mental impairment that (1) has lasted (or is expected to last) at least 1 year or is expected to result in death and (2) prevents them from engaging in substantial gainful activity, defined as work activity that involves significant physical or mental activities performed for pay or profit. RRB's policy states that, to establish eligibility for financial benefits, examiners should assess medical records for evidence that a claimant is too severely disabled to maintain gainful employment, and establish that a claimant's earnings fall below a certain threshold. However, the procedure for establishing if claimants meet the income threshold relies on SSA earnings data that can be up to 1 year old. Sources of more timely earnings information, such as the Department of Health and Human Services' National Directory of New Hires and *The Work Number*, exist and include both non-railroad and self-employment earnings, but RRB has not sufficiently explored the possibility of using them to help establish eligibility for T&P disability benefits. In addition, RRB lacks a policy to require independent supervisory review for all claims determinations. As a result, the procedures that claims examiners use to review a claim also allow them sole discretion to decide whether to approve it. Between 2008 and 2012, RRB data show that about one-quarter to one-third of T&P claims are considered and approved without independent supervisory review. According to generally accepted standards for internal controls in the federal government, essential tasks—such as establishing and determining that benefits should be awarded—should be performed by separate individuals to reduce the risk of fraud.

RRB's strategy for post-eligibility quality assurance review is inadequate to ensure that disability determinations for approved claims are accurate and does not address program risks due to potential fraud. While RRB checks the accuracy of payment amounts, and periodically reviews compliance with its policies, it does not evaluate the accuracy of disability determinations made or regularly monitor the effectiveness of the determination process. Similarly, performance goals for the disability program focus on measures of timeliness and do not track the accuracy of determinations made. The agency also has not engaged in a comprehensive effort to continuously identify fraud within the program, even after a high-profile incident exposed fraud as a key program risk. RRB has conducted some analyses to identify patterns in claims data that may suggest potential fraud, but the work has not led to new practices in the T&P program. Finally, while RRB officials stated that the agency has developed and provided some fraud awareness training, staff in all four of the district offices that GAO interviewed did not recall receiving this training, and some stated that it was not their responsibility to be alert for potential fraud, further limiting RRB's ability to ensure it is paying benefits only to eligible claimants.

Contents

Abbreviations

CDR	continuing disability review
DI	Disability Insurance
LIRR	Long Island Rail Road
MEF	Master Earnings File
NDNH	National Directory of New Hires
OASI	Old-Age and Survivors Insurance
OIG	Office of the Inspector General
PER	preeffectuation review
QA	Quality Assurance
RRA	Railroad Retirement Act of 1974
RRB	Railroad Retirement Board
SSA	Social Security Administration
SSEB	Social Security Equivalent Benefit
T&P	total and permanent

GAO
U.S. GOVERNMENT ACCOUNTABILITY OFFICE
441 G St. N.W.
Washington, DC 20548

June 26, 2014

The Honorable Sam Johnson
Chairman
Subcommittee on Social Security
Committee on Ways and Means
House of Representatives

Dear Mr. Chairman,

The U.S. Railroad Retirement Board (RRB) is responsible for administering retirement, survivor, and disability benefits for railroad workers and their families under the Railroad Retirement Act of 1974 (RRA).[1] Although RRB administers its programs separately from those administered by the Social Security Administration (SSA), both RRB and SSA share jurisdiction over the payment of railroad worker benefits. In fiscal year 2012, RRB paid almost $276 million in total and permanent (T&P) disability benefits to about 12,970 beneficiaries with physical or mental impairments that prevent them from performing any type of work.

In recent years, RRB has been the subject of Inspector General, Government Accountability Office (GAO), and SSA audits, which have disclosed weaknesses in RRB's internal controls and oversight of its benefit programs. These audits have found problems with basic RRB operations and procedures, as well as higher-level deficiencies in RRB's oversight process. Additionally, between the late 1990s and 2008, as many as 1,500 former Long Island Rail Road (LIRR) workers, with the assistance of several medical doctors, a former union official, and a former RRB field office manager, were suspected of falsely claiming RRB benefits which if paid in full could total more than $1 billion—exceeding the total amount of benefits paid to all claimants in fiscal year 2012— underscoring the need for effective program oversight. To date, 28 individuals have pled guilty and 5 were convicted in federal court. These actions have resulted in approximately $400 million in restitution and forfeiture. An additional 44 individuals also voluntarily disclosed their involvement in the fraud scheme and agreed to the termination of their RRB disability benefits. In light of these issues, we examined the

---

[1] Pub. L. No. 93-445, 88 Stat. 1305, codified at 45 U.S.C. § 231 et seq.

GAO-14-418 Railroad Retirement Board

oversight and management controls of RRB's T&P benefit program. Specifically, this report examines:

1. whether RRB's policies and procedures are adequate to ensure that only eligible claimants receive total and permanent disability benefits, and
2. the extent to which RRB's management strategy ensures that determinations are accurate and addresses program risks.

To address these objectives, we reviewed RRB's policies and procedures for processing railroad workers' T&P claims using standards defined within the RRA, and GAO's published standards for internal control. We interviewed RRB managers and staff at headquarters and in four district offices— Jacksonville, Florida; Billings, Montana; Westbury, New York; and Fort Worth, Texas—to learn how disability claims were processed. In addition, we reviewed a nongeneralizable random sample of 10 RRB only approved T&P cases approved in fiscal year 2012, to test for potential vulnerabilities with the program's management controls over cases that were decided by RRB. Using GAO's *Standards for Internal Control in the Federal Government* and relevant federal law,[2] we evaluated RRB's management strategies and tools, and the extent to which they provided the agency with a comprehensive picture of the effectiveness of its process and program performance. We also reviewed prior reports by GAO, RRB management, RRB and SSA Offices of Inspector General (OIG); and reviewed the information that RRB uses to manage its claims process. We assessed the reliability of RRB-provided T&P and continuing disability review (CDR) data by (1) reviewing existing information about the data and the system that produced them, and (2) interviewing agency officials knowledgeable about the data. We determined that the data were sufficiently reliable for the purposes of this report. We conducted this performance audit from February 2013 to June 2014 in accordance with generally accepted government auditing standards. Those standards require that we plan and perform the audit to obtain sufficient, appropriate evidence to provide a reasonable basis for our findings and conclusions based on our audit objectives. We believe that the evidence obtained provides a reasonable basis for our findings and conclusions based on our audit objectives.

---

[2] GAO, *Standards for Internal Control in the Federal Government*, GAO/AIMD-00-21.3.1 (Washington, D.C., Nov. 1, 1999). GAO/AIMD-00-21.3.1.

Background

Under the Railroad Retirement Act of 1974, RRB makes independent determinations of railroad workers' claimed T&P disability using the same general criteria that SSA uses to administer its Disability Insurance (DI) program—that is, the worker must have a medically determinable physical or mental impairment that (1) has lasted (or is expected to last) at least 1 year or is expected to result in death and (2) prevents them from engaging in substantial gainful activity, defined as work activity that involves significant physical or mental activities performed for pay or profit.[3] Railroad workers determined to be eligible for benefits under the T&P program are not expected to be able to return to the workforce. The eligibility criteria for the T&P disability program differ from those of the RRB's occupational disability program.[4] Workers determined to be eligible for benefits under the occupational disability program may be able return to the workforce, but generally may not return to their original occupation. T&P disability benefits are payable to employees with at least 10 years (120 months) of creditable railroad service or to employees with 5 years (60 months) of creditable railroad service after 1995. SSA staff review about one-third of the cases that RRB has determined to be eligible for T&P benefits for which Social Security benefits may potentially be paid. In fiscal year 2012, RRB made 1,254 initial determinations under T&P standards. Of these initial determinations, 977 were approved for benefits.

Claims representatives—staff located in RRB's 53 field offices—assemble applications, and collect individuals' employment and medical information needed to support the claim. Once assembled, claims representatives send the files to RRB headquarters for processing, and program eligibility determination. Claims examiners—staff located in RRB headquarters—review the case file documentation and periodically order additional medical examinations to determine whether a railroad worker is eligible for T&P benefits. RRB uses the same definition of disability and evaluates T&P claims using the same criteria SSA uses for the DI program. For

---

[3] For T&P criteria, see 45 U.S.C. § 231a(a)(1)(v) and 20 C.F.R. §§ 220.26, 220.28, and 220.141. For DI criteria, see 42 U.S.C. § 423(d)(1) and 20 C.F.R. § 404.1572.

[4] The occupational disability program—which uses labor-and management-negotiated disability criteria that apply only to a worker's' ability to perform his or her specific railroad occupation—provides benefits for workers who have physical or mental impairments that prevent them from performing their specific railroad job, regardless of whether they can perform other work. For example, a railroad engineer who cannot frequently climb, bend, and reach, as required by the job, may be found occupationally disabled.

GAO-14-418 Railroad Retirement Board

example, RRB determines whether the claimant's impairment is medically disabling. If the claims examiner determines that a claimant has an impairment that meets or equals SSA's Listing of Impairments (which describes medical conditions that SSA has determined are severe enough to keep the claimant from performing any type of work), the examiner will find that the claimant is disabled. If the claimant's impairment is not found medically disabling, RRB then determines whether the claimant is able to do his or her past work, or potentially any other work.

Together, RRB and SSA coordinate the financing of T&P disability benefits,[5] which totaled almost $276 million in fiscal year 2012.[6] Doing so involves computing the amount of Social Security payroll taxes that would have been collected by certain Social Security Trust Funds if railroad employment had been covered directly by Social Security, as well as the amount of additional benefits which Social Security would have paid to railroad retirement beneficiaries during the same fiscal year. When benefits exceed payroll taxes, the difference, including interest and administrative expenses, is transferred from the Social Security Trust Funds to the RRB's Social Security Equivalent Benefit Account.[7] If taxes exceed benefit reimbursements, a transfer is made in favor of the Social Security Trust Funds. However, since 1959, such transfers have favored RRB. In the last month of fiscal year 2012, Social Security trust funds financed about 79 percent of total T&P disability benefits (see fig. 1).

---

[5] This is accomplished through the financial interchange process, which provides for a yearly transfer of funds between RRB and SSA trust fund accounts.

[6] The $276 million in fiscal year 2012 is based on information from RRB stating that the average monthly annuity was $1,773 for the 12,970 individuals in current payment status.

[7] The Social Security Equivalent Benefit (SSEB) Account, which is separate from other railroad retirement accounts, is used to record revenues and pay Social Security equivalent benefits. Funds in the SSEB Account are used to pay Social Security equivalent benefits and related expenses. A Social Security equivalent benefit is the portion of a railroad retirement annuity that corresponds to an amount calculated under Social Security formulas, but is based on combined railroad and Social Security credits.

GAO-14-418 Railroad Retirement Board

Figure 1: Relative Amounts of Total and Permanent Disability Benefits Paid to Those under Full Retirement Age from Different Trust Fund Accounts, September 2012

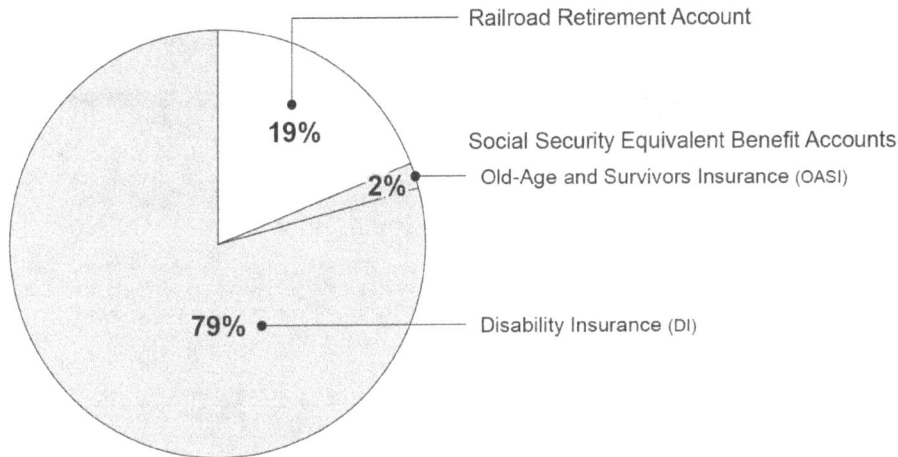

Source: Information provided by Railroad Retirement Board (RRB).

Note: According to RRB officials, the Social Security Equivalent Benefit Account also receives taxes, and the SSA financial interchange pays only the costs that exceed these other financing sources. In fiscal year 2012, the financial interchange—along with SSA and the Centers for Medicare and Medicaid Services—provided about 38 percent of financing for all benefits (not just T&P disability benefits) paid from the Railroad Retirement and Social Security Equivalent Benefit Accounts.

Once the T&P disability benefit has been awarded, RRB uses continuing disability reviews (CDRs) to determine whether beneficiaries remain eligible for benefits.[8] These reviews can include a determination of whether an individual's medical condition has improved to the point where he or she is no longer considered disabled, is capable of performing work (whether or not that work involves railroad employment) or whether the individual continues to earn income below allowable program limits. In fiscal year 2012, RRB completed 1,212 CDR activities.[9]

---

[8] The general requirements for initiating CDRs are provided at 20 C.F.R. § 220.186. RRB initiates additional CDRs at their discretion.

[9] RRB does not differentiate between T&P and occupational disability when tracking CDRs. Including other types of CDR activities, such as mailed questionnaires, RRB completed 1,212 CDR activities in fiscal year 2012. Claimants are permitted to earn other income while receiving benefits, however, the amount of allowable income is capped at $10,500, after deduction of disability-related work expenses.

GAO-14-418 Railroad Retirement Board

The T&P disability program is linked to RRB's occupational disability program, in that claimants use the same application and medical evidence to apply for benefits under both programs. Figure 2 shows RRB's disability T&P claims determination process, including how this process relates to the occupational disability claims process.

Figure 2: RRB's Total and Permanent Disability Determination Process

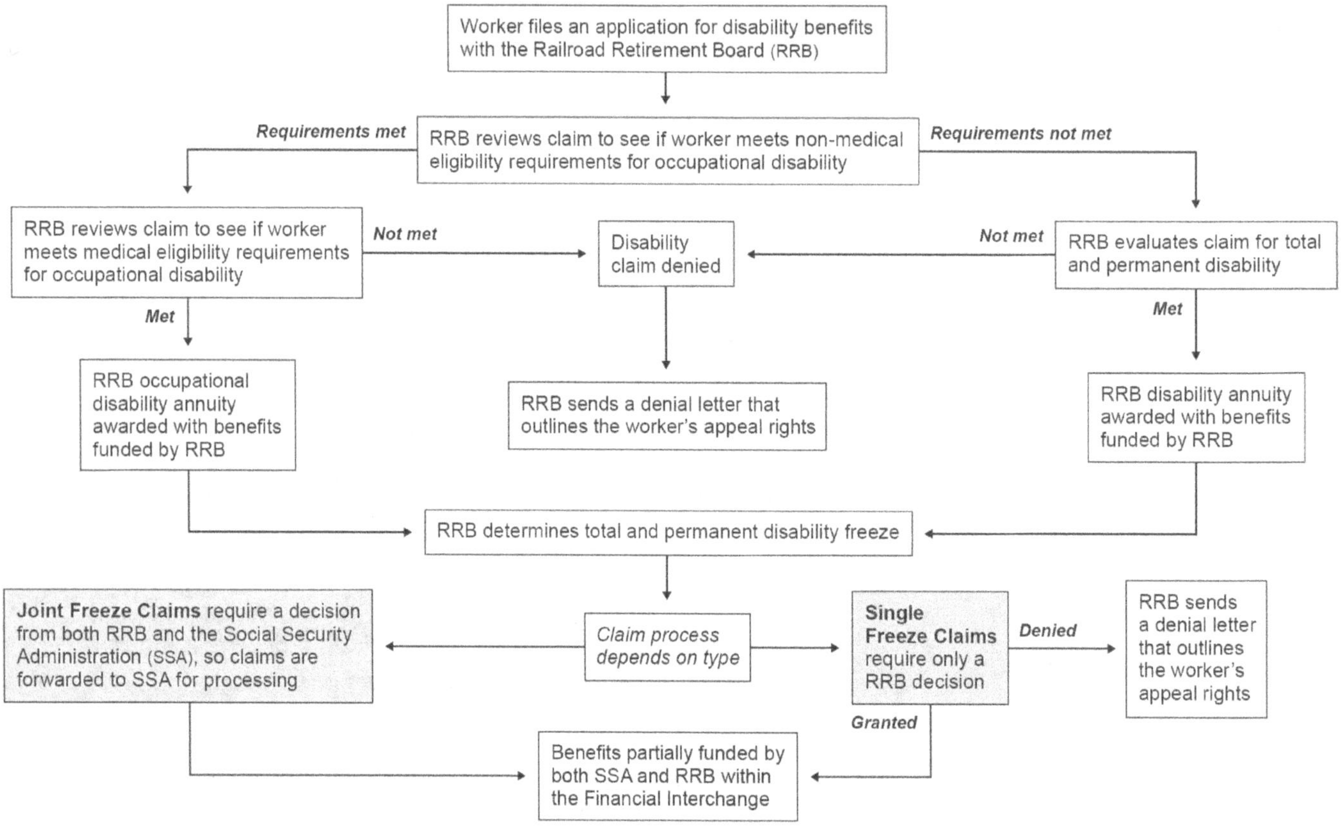

Source: GAO analysis of SSA Office of Inspector General report: Quick Response Evaluation: Processing of Railroad Worker Disability Claims (A-05-09-29119). | GAO-14-418

In response to the LIRR fraud incident, RRB implemented a five point-plan to increase its oversight of LIRR employees who file for occupational disability benefits or who are currently receiving occupational disability benefits. Under the five point-plan, RRB:

1. orders its own medical exams for all LIRR claimants to supplement medical evidence provided,

2. conducts continuing disability reviews for all LIRR occupational disability annuitants age 54.5 and younger (as of October 21, 2008),

3. exercises greater oversight of its Westbury field office in Long Island through biweekly phone calls and quarterly visits,

4. collects and plans to analyze data for LIRR claims to detect any unusual patterns, such as impairments and treating physicians that appear more frequently, and

5. collects data on the extent to which LIRR management employees are applying for benefits under the program.

In March 2013, RRB reported that a review of 519 occupational disability applications for LIRR employees being handled under the plan resulted in 496 of the applications being granted—an approval rate of about 96 percent.[10] According to the RRB OIG, the approval rate of LIRR occupational disability applicants remains essentially unchanged from when the LIRR fraud incident was made public and is indicative of systemic problems within the program.

---

[10] RRB reported that 3 of the 522 LIRR occupational disability applications being handled in accordance with the Five-Point Plan were withdrawn.

Policies and Procedures for Awarding Total and Permanent Disability Benefits Are Not Adequate to Ensure Proper Payments

Evidence Used to Establish Eligibility May Be Inadequate

The procedures RRB uses to verify a claimant's work and earnings and the severity and duration of physical or mental impairments are inadequate to ensure that only eligible claimants qualify for T&P benefits. *Standards for Internal Control in the Federal Government* states that agencies should ensure that all transactions and other significant events are clearly documented. This would include determinations that claimants are entitled to benefits under the RRA. Such documentation could facilitate tracing these actions from initiation through completion of the final claim determination.[11] Therefore, current and complete information about a claimant's work and earnings history and alleged impairment is critical to establishing not only whether claimants are eligible for benefits, but also the correct benefit amount to be paid.

RRB relies on earnings data that can be up to 1 year old and may exclude other sources of income that can help establish whether a claimant is engaged in substantial gainful activity. To establish eligibility for T&P benefits, RRB requires claimants to disclose their work for the current and past 15 calendar years, and earnings from the current and preceding calendar year, including earnings from self-employment.[12] RRB verifies the claimant's work and earnings history through a detailed query of the claimant's reported earnings, as recorded in SSA's Master

---

[11] GAO/AIMD-00-21.3.1.

[12] Claimants must list all jobs that they had in the 15 years before they stopped working, and describe their duties and weekly hours of work. The list does not include earnings for these jobs.

Earnings File (MEF).[13] However, the most recent earnings information contained within the MEF are for the last complete calendar year, and as a result, the data that RRB uses to determine eligibility may lag behind actual earnings by up to 12 months.

Although RRB requires that claims examiners perform a detailed query of reported earnings in the MEF at the time of their initial determination, our review of case files showed that some determinations were based on data that were as much as 10 months old. Three of the 10 case files we reviewed also did not include sufficient information to allow us to determine what additional steps, if any, were taken to verify that earnings in the year the claims were filed did not exceed program limits. In one of the case files, the claims examiner appeared to rely solely on the claimant's statement that there were no current earnings and in two others, the claimant provided no information on current year earnings. In discussing this issue, RRB officials noted that claims examiners routinely perform an electronic query of the MEF before a claim is approved for payment but may neglect to subsequently include a printout of the query in the case file. Regardless of this explanation, the absence of this documentation made it difficult to confirm that such queries were performed. As a result, without complete documentation of all evidence used to arrive at the initial determination, RRB lacks the ability to provide reasonable assurance that these determinations are being made in accordance with RRB policies and comply with relevant regulations.

Although more current information on work and earnings are available, RRB has not explored these sources of information for T&P claims. According to RRB, its annual match of current RRB beneficiaries against the MEF, which helps target cases for CDRs, could help flag earnings that may go undetected prior to an initial claim being awarded. However, RRB has not reviewed this information to determine if the time lag for reported earnings has resulted in the award of ineligible claims or potential overpayments. In addition, the Department of Health and Human Services' National Directory of New Hires (NDNH)—established in part to

---

[13] The MEF is a database of earnings maintained by SSA that includes earnings for individuals as reported to SSA by employers on Form W-2 (Wage and Tax Statement), and income from self-employment as reported to the IRS on Schedule SE. Although RRB maintains its own data system for monitoring railroad employment income and related taxes, the system does not include work and earnings from non-railroad employment or self-employment.

help states enforce child support orders against noncustodial parents—contains quarterly state wage information which is also more recent than the annual wage information included in the MEF.[14] The NDNH also includes data from state directories of new hires, state records of unemployment insurance benefits paid, and federal agency payroll data, all of which can be used to help establish a more recent picture of a claimant's work and earnings. Access to the NDNH is limited by statute. Although RRB does not have specific legal authority to access it, RRB has considered obtaining access to the NDNH for the purpose of fraud prevention in its unemployment and sickness benefit programs, but abandoned the effort, citing cost as a key reason for not pursuing it further.[15] In May 2011, the agency revisited the issue in the wake of the LIRR fraud incident. Specifically, in May 2011, RRB studied the feasibility of using the NDNH to monitor the earnings level of individuals who are already receiving disability benefits. RRB concluded that it would not provide significant benefits due to costs associated with accessing the database and redesigning its processes; the need for legislation to grant RRB access; and potentially higher workloads, but did not quantify the potential financial benefits. Furthermore, the study did not address whether it would be cost-effective to use the NDNH to obtain more current information about the earnings of people who apply for benefits. SSA, which has legal authority to access the NDNH, currently uses the NDNH to periodically monitor the earnings of those receiving Supplemental Security Income benefits,[16] and to investigate the current, or recent alleged work activity that is not yet posted to the MEF for DI applicants and beneficiaries.[17] Other tools for verifying claimants' earnings may be

---

[14] The Secretary of Health and Human Services is required to establish and maintain the NDNH within the Federal Parent Locator Service. 42 U.S.C. § 653(i).

[15] RRB officials told us that in 1999 they decided to seek an amendment granting such authority, but that the amendment was never enacted and RRB withdrew the proposal from its 2006 legislative program.

[16] SSA's Supplemental Security Income program provides cash assistance for eligible aged, blind, and disabled individuals with limited financial means.

[17] Although SSA currently lacks the ability to perform batch queries of the NDNH to help monitor the earnings of all DI beneficiaries, it is conducting a cost-benefit analysis to explore the feasibility of gaining access for this purpose.

available from the public sector, such as *The Work Number*—a commercial, publicly-available data source.[18]

RRB procedures provide claims staff flexibility to decide when to verify medical evidence. Field office claims representatives are responsible for assembling claim files and ensuring they are complete before forwarding them to headquarters for evaluation; however, RRB does not require them to verify that medical evidence is obtained from a reliable source. Specifically, RRB's field operations manual advises claims representatives to "make no judgment as to the acceptability of a medical source" and that, in the unlikely situation that the only medical-related evidence is from a source considered unacceptable, a headquarters claims examiner is to direct any further development of medical evidence.[19] However, RRB's guidance to headquarters claims examiners notes that most claimants have impairments that are either continuing or worsening, and directs them to avoid unnecessary claims development.[20] RRB procedures require that claims representatives and examiners order consultative medical examinations when necessary to help determine the severity of a medical condition and the guidance provides for discretion when deciding whether such steps are warranted. Consequently, most of the field staff we spoke with across district offices indicated that the degree to which evidence is complete before sending the case forward varies from case to case. For example, claims representatives in one district office reported that if an application does not include medical records, they will request a medical examination before forwarding the claim to headquarters. In another field office, claims representatives said that if medical evidence is missing, they typically will forward the

---

[18] *The Work Number* is a commercial service provided by Equifax that allows social service organizations and others to locate an individual's current place of employment or uncover unreported income, based on the most recent payroll data from over 2,500 employers nationwide. Inquiries may be made individually, or through automated data matches. The information is limited to employers who participate in the system.

[19] *RRB Field Operations Manual*, 1305.35.2.

[20] *RRB Disability Claims Manual*, 4.3.7, states: "Most claimants have impairments which are by nature either static or progressive and, therefore, significant improvement within 12 months is not expected. Since severity is the main issue in such cases, most can be documented and evaluated immediately. Avoid unnecessary development. For instance, if the impairment has already been found to be severe and it is of a chronic or progressive nature, care must be taken to establish that the duration requirement is met and the onset date is correct if it differs from the claimant's alleged onset date."

application to headquarters with an annotation asking that medical examinations be ordered by the appropriate claims examiner.

Although claims representatives are a potentially valuable source of first-hand information about individuals filing T&P claims, and often represent the agency's sole direct contact with claimants, our interviews and review of claims files showed that claims representatives' observations are used infrequently. When compiling case files, claims representatives can include comments in designated parts of the application form, the customer contact log, or in the form used to transmit the file to headquarters. For example, a claimant who reports having a condition that prevents them from walking without assistance could be observed walking without a cane, or a claimant may present evidence of being unable to sleep without mentioning associated behaviors such as memory loss or difficulty concentrating that are clearly evident to the claims reviewer. However, of the 10 cases we reviewed, 1 included remarks from a claims representative documenting observations about the claimant's physical symptoms and another included observations regarding possible self-employment that the claimant had denied. In a third case, the transmittal notes appear to have been added after the claim had already been transmitted. RRB's online customer contact log, used to track all interactions with claimants, can also be used to record observations, including whether observed behavior contradicts medical evidence. Although claims representatives and district managers said that field staff may record their observations about the claimant in customer contact logs, claims examiners told us that they review these remarks only for the purpose of determining whether there is further evidence to be forwarded. According to staff in the Westbury district office, a formal process for flagging suspicious medical evidence may have allowed the agency to flag potentially fraudulent claims from LIRR workers for additional scrutiny by claims examiners.

RRB Policies and Procedures Do Not Ensure Initial Claims Are Properly Reviewed

RRB policies and procedures do not require that all initial determinations are reviewed by an independent person to ensure that there is sufficient evidence to support the determination. *Standards for Internal Control in the Federal Government* states that agencies should ensure that key duties and responsibilities are divided or segregated among different people to reduce the risk of error, waste, or fraud.[21] However, RRB's policies and procedures allow for discretion at the field office level

---

[21] GAO/AIMD-00-21.3.1.

regarding how complete the case file must be before it is forwarded to headquarters for a determination, and these files are subject to different levels of supervisory review. Some district managers stated that they make a point of reviewing virtually all claims developed in their offices before they are mailed to headquarters, while others review only a required sample of 10 percent of all claims, including those for other RRB benefit programs, chiefly due to workload volume or competing duties.[22] In our review of case files, we observed that required information, such as the year that a claimant last attended school or when the application was signed, was missing from 4 of the 10 applications in the physical files we reviewed. In another case, the medical evidence was over 12 months old and new evidence was not developed, as required. Incomplete case file information raises questions about whether all the relevant information was properly considered in these cases.

At the determination level, RRB policy allows for some claims to be approved without independent supervisory review. RRB policies generally allow examiners to use their judgment to decide which cases do not require independent review because an individual's ailment meets or exceeds SSA's listing of impairments.[23] For such claims, a single RRB claims examiner can self-authorize the claim. Consequently, in recent years, about one-quarter to one-third of all T&P initial claims were approved by the same claims examiner that reviewed the application (see fig. 3). Such claims may be problematic if there is an error in judgment on the part of the claims examiner.

---

[22] Some district managers also serve as network managers. Network managers are responsible for disseminating training or other information to several district offices within a defined geographic area, and for helping to balance workloads among the offices in their network.

[23] According to SSA, to conclude that a condition meets or exceeds this listing, there must be sufficient evidence to show that the claimant has an impairment that is severe enough to prevent him or her from performing any gainful activity. (See 20 C.F.R. § 404.1525.) Additional criteria for handling other types of claims without authorization are provided at *RRB Disability Claims Manual*, 3.4.304.

Figure 3: Percent of Self-Authorized Total and Permanent Initial Determinations, Fiscal Years 2008-2012

Total and permanent (T&P) disability determinations

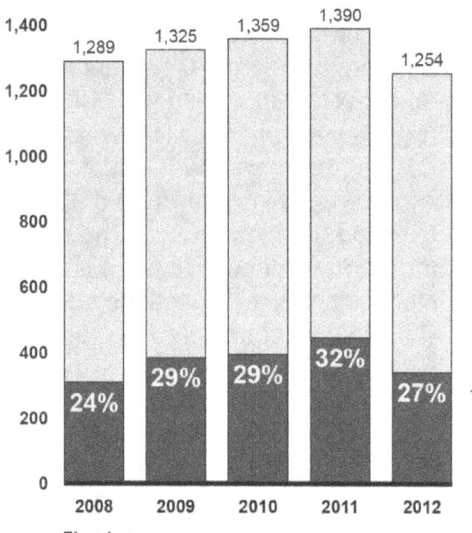

◄ Percentage of those determinations that were self-authorized

Source: GAO analysis of Railroad Retirement Board (RRB) data as reported in Compliance Evaluation of Initial Disability Cases Where Authorization is Not Required, Report No. 12-7, April 20, 2012 (2008-2011), and as provided by RRB (2012).

Note: Fiscal year 2012 data were extracted based on search criteria that may be incomparable with data for FY2008-11. In addition, these data are not limited to employee T&P determinations but include determinations for other applicants, such as a spouse with a disabled child, a widow(er) or other surviving dependent.

RRB's Management Strategy Does Not Ensure That Total and Permanent Disability Determinations Are Accurate and Does Not Adequately Address Potential Fraud

Program Oversight Has Not Ensured the Quality of Disability Determinations

RRB's T&P program oversight process does not evaluate the accuracy of disability determinations or provide managers with regular feedback about the effectiveness of the determination process. According to RRB's strategic plan and agency officials, RRB's key program objectives are to make accurate and timely determinations and payments, and to pay accurate benefits to eligible claimants. RRB's Program Evaluation and Management Services periodically conducts reviews of selected aspects of the T&P program; however, rather than providing routine feedback about the quality and accuracy of the determination process, these evaluations are narrowly focused and according to RRB officials, generally examine compliance with procedures and guidance. RRB's oversight is primarily focused on checking the accuracy of payment amounts, periodically reviewing policy compliance, and assessing the continued eligibility of already approved beneficiaries using CDRs and death record matching. While RRB conducts annual reviews of benefit accuracy,[24] these reviews only measure the percentage of dollars paid correctly and do not evaluate whether the medical evidence supported the claimed disability or whether the process RRB used to establish eligibility led to an accurate determination. Occasionally, the division conducts full reviews of selected determinations, including the medical evidence; however, such reviews have been conducted on an ad hoc basis for internal purposes, have taken place after payments were

---

[24] The review includes all benefits authorized under the RRA and T&P cases are included in the sample of cases reviewed.

initiated, and have focused on certain types of determinations, such as self-authorized claims.[25] *Standards for Internal Control in the Federal Government* states that agency management should assess and continually monitor program performance to provide reasonable assurance that the agency is achieving its objectives.[26] According to RRB officials, the CDR program is the agency's response to major program integrity issues identified in the T&P program—though the number of work and medical CDRs completed has declined in recent years. For example, in fiscal year 2009, RRB conducted 610 work and medical CDRs; however, that number had declined to 235 in fiscal year 2012 (see fig. 4).

Figure 4: RRB Continuing Disability Reviews, Fiscal Years 2008-2012

Number of continuing disability reviews (CDRs) completed

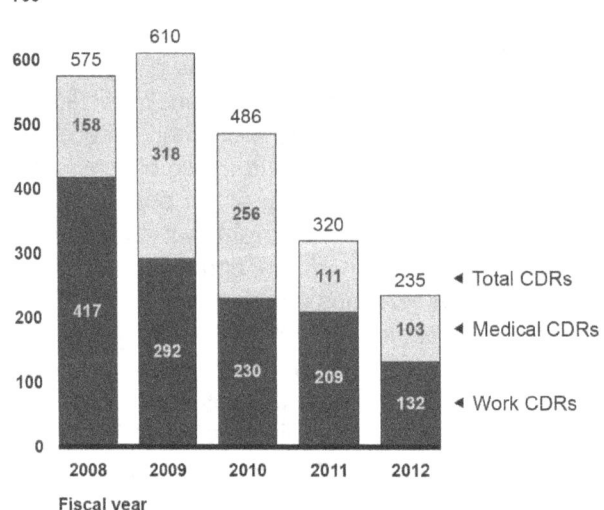

Source: GAO analysis of Railroad Retirement Board data.

---

[25] Two example reports are *Compliance Evaluation of Activities of Daily Living Procedures* (RRB report number A&T 09-09, released 5/12/09) and *Compliance Evaluation of Initial Disability Cases Where Authorization is not Required* (RRB report number A&T 10-14, released 5/21/10; RRB report number PEMS 12-7, released 4/26/12).

[26] GAO/AIMD-00-21.3.1.

According to RRB officials, the decline was, in part, a result of a corresponding decline in the number of staff reviewers.[27]

In contrast to RRB, SSA monitors quality in its similar DI program by reviewing samples of disability determinations for accuracy prior to initiating benefit payments. SSA's Office of Quality Review, which is in a separate division from initial claims examiners, conducts two types of quality assurance reviews prior to initiating disability payments: (1) ongoing quality assurance (QA) reviews, and (2) preeffectuation (PER) reviews, which are intended to detect and correct improper disability determinations prior to benefits being paid. For its QA review, SSA pulls a random sample of 70 determinations and 70 denials per calendar quarter per state. For its PER review, SSA pulls a sample of cases predicted to be most likely to contain errors and represents 50 percent of all disability approvals. For both reviews, QA staff evaluate the sampled cases to ensure that the medical evidence supports the claimed disability and that the evidence and the determination conform to SSA operating policies and procedures. QA staff then communicate any errors and determination reversals to the initial examiners and use the information collected, including how and where errors occurred, to provide general feedback on program performance.[28]

The lack of routine up-front reviews of determination accuracy and the quality of the determination process leaves RRB at risk of paying benefits to ineligible individuals. One RRB official attributed RRB's lack of such oversight to the agency's belief that delaying benefits to conduct accuracy reviews before sending the payment would be detrimental to customer service. According to OIG officials, RRB places greater focus on paying benefits than with ensuring benefits are warranted, and noted that if RRB strengthened its quality assurance framework prior to disability approval and payment, fewer improper claims would be awarded. RRB does not publicly report its approval rate for disability claims in its annual performance and accountability report; however, as noted above, RRB

---

[27] RRB does not differentiate between T&P and occupational disability when tracking CDRs. Including other types of CDR activities, such as medical improvement possible (MIP) mailed questionnaires, the total number of CDRs declined annually from 2,850 in fiscal year 2009 to 1,212 in fiscal year 2012.

[28] In fiscal year 2013, SSA conducted 31,672 QA reviews and 333,159 PER reviews, and found errors or inadequate documentation in 608 (1.9 percent) and 9,619 (2.9 percent), respectively.

approved benefits in 78 percent of T&P cases decided in fiscal year 2012 (977 of 1,254).

RRB also lacks agency-wide performance goals that emphasize the importance of determination accuracy. Specifically, RRB has established performance goals that track the timeliness of disability determinations and payments, but has not established goals that track whether the right people are being awarded benefits over time.[29] Federal law requires that agencies establish outcome-related goals and objectives that relate to key agency priorities.[30] For the T&P program, RRB's strategic goals focus on the accuracy of payment calculations, the timeliness of the disability determination process, and the timeliness of payments. However, RRB's performance goals do not measure or track the accuracy of disability determinations—in other words, whether benefits are being correctly awarded or denied. In its similar DI program, SSA has a performance goal that tracks the accuracy rate for initial disability determinations over time, in addition to goals that track timeliness. SSA's accuracy rate goal measures the percentage of determinations that contained errors as identified during their regular quality assurance process reviews, and SSA sets its fiscal year 2013 target accuracy rate at 97 percent. Without similarly tracking and reporting on the accuracy of T&P disability determinations in addition to measuring payment accuracy and timeliness, RRB does not know whether it is paying benefits only to eligible individuals and cannot observe trends over time.

RRB Has Not Engaged in a Comprehensive Effort to Continuously Identify and Prevent Fraud System-wide

RRB has not engaged in a comprehensive effort to continuously identify and prevent potential fraud program-wide even after the high-profile LIRR incident exposed fraud as a key program risk. Fraud that has occurred in the occupational disability program may suggest a broader risk of fraud in RRB's disability programs because medical documentation in a claimant's case file may be used to justify either occupational or T&P benefits. According to OIG officials, doctors often document occupational

---

[29] RRB's publicly reported performance measures provide some information about the accuracy of initial recurring retirement payments, which includes whether all annuities, including T&P benefits, are calculated correctly. It also provides limited information about the timeliness of the T&P program because it aggregates data on all disability determinations, not just T&P. Over the past 5 fiscal years (2008-2012), the timeliness of T&P determinations has consistently been about 12-13 percentage points lower than the overall measure.

[30] 5 U.S.C. § 306(a)(2).

disabilities in such a way that a claimant would also qualify for the T&P program. In addition, RRB officials stated that, while randomly assigning claims for examination at headquarters is intended to prevent collusion between examiners and claims representatives in the field offices, it also limits the ability of examiners to recognize patterns of potential fraud, which RRB officials noted was made apparent by the LIRR incident. Since that incident, RRB has increased its scrutiny of claims from LIRR workers—for example, by ordering more consultative medical exams. However, its other actions to improve fraud awareness and prevention have been limited and narrowly focused. RRB hired an analyst to conduct ongoing reviews of agency data to identify patterns that suggest potential fraud, but the analyst's work has thus far been focused on the occupational disability program. In 2011, RRB also conducted an analysis of 89 cases of proven fraud in its occupational and T&P disability programs to identify common characteristics that could aid in identifying at-risk cases earlier in the process,[31] but RRB did not draw any conclusions about new ways to identify potential fraud and, as a result, did not make any system-wide changes to the determination process. RRB officials stated that this work was not intended to lead to changes in the process, but to identify other areas for examination. In addition, while OIG officials said they have encouraged RRB staff to refer suspicious claims to the OIG's office before approving disability benefits—instead of chasing the benefit in a subsequent fraud investigation—RRB has not referred any suspicious claims to the OIG in the year and a half since that guidance was provided.

RRB's efforts to identify and prevent potential fraud have been limited and are focused primarily on claims submitted by LIRR workers, which may leave RRB's T&P program vulnerable to risks of fraud. *Standards for Internal Control in the Federal Government* states that agencies should identify program risks from both internal and external sources, analyze possible effects, and take action to manage the risks.[32] According to RRB officials, since the LIRR incident, the agency has become highly alert to potential abuse and is in the process of evaluating and implementing safety measures. However, OIG officials stated that RRB's process for

---

[31] In this context, cases of proven fraud are from a list of cases that, according to the RRB OIG, had been successfully prosecuted for fraud as a result of undisclosed employment while receiving disability benefits from RRB.

[32] GAO/AIMD-00-21.3.1.

reviewing medical evidence and making disability determinations still does not allow RRB to effectively identify potential medical fraud because the agency does not have sufficient medical expertise on staff and the process does not include reviews of initial determinations by independent doctors. According to RRB officials, the 10 cases we reviewed included 8 that had been reviewed by SSA's medical experts and 2 that had been sent to the RRB's medical contractors. While 8 of the case files we reviewed contained copies of SSA's own disability determinations that were reviewed by SSA's doctors, the same case files did not contain evidence that SSA doctors had reviewed RRB's T&P disability determinations.

Moreover, RRB management has not fostered an environment of fraud awareness throughout the agency. While RRB has initiated fraud awareness training, agency participation has been incomplete and updates and refreshers have been sporadic. The training program has included instructor-led sessions for headquarters staff and recorded modules for field service personnel. According to RRB, 59 of about 566 headquarters staff completed fraud awareness training in 2011, including all members of the Disability Benefits Division, and all 53 field offices reported viewing the recorded program.[33] However, claims representatives in all four of the district offices that we contacted said they had not received any training directly related to fraud awareness. RRB officials stated that they relied on manager certification that the training was completed in 2011 and thought that staff we interviewed may have forgotten about the training since it was more than 2 years ago. After learning of our findings, RRB officials issued a directive to all network managers to confirm by March 2014 that all field staff had completed fraud awareness training. According to RRB, 29 claims examiners and analysts at headquarters also participated in a two-part class that revisited fraud topics in 2013; however, this follow-up course was not offered to field offices. In addition, agency officials stated that RRB's fraud awareness training has been *ad hoc* and that no annual refresher courses are required of, or have been offered to staff. In addition to the training courses, RRB officials stated that they distributed a twice-yearly newsletter intended to heighten fraud awareness. The newsletters provide examples of disability fraud in the news and links to the OIG website, but do not include messages from management or information regarding other training resources. Despite RRB's efforts, claims

---

[33] Staff in RRB headquarters excludes the OIG.

representatives in two of the four district offices we contacted said that it was not their job to be on the lookout for potential fraud. For example, one claims representative said that even if something suspicious appears on an application and a claimant has signed the application, the claims representative has no responsibility to draw attention to the suspicious information since it is the responsibility of headquarters' staff to evaluate claimants' answers. In addition, a district manager from the same office stated that even when faced with obvious patterns of potentially fraudulent activity in the past, claims representatives had no mechanism by which to flag the issue and generally have not been encouraged to do so. Without agency-wide commitment to be alert to potential fraud, including having the tools and training to identify suspicious claims, RRB may not have sufficient information or context to make accurate disability determinations and improper payments may result.

Conclusions

The RRB's total and permanent disability program provides an important safety net for individuals who are unable to work due to a disability. The program provided $276 million in benefits to 12,970 beneficiaries in fiscal year 2012 alone. While our review shows that RRB has taken some steps to address potential fraud within the program, its existing policies and processes impede its ability to prevent improper payments or to detect and prevent fraudulent claims system-wide. In particular, RRB's continued reliance on outdated earnings information to identify beneficiaries who may not be eligible for benefits, or on insufficient medical evidence to make accurate initial determinations means that the agency cannot ensure it is able to detect and prevent improper payments including some that can potentially be very large. As a result, RRB has placed itself in a "pay and chase" mode that stretches limited staff and budgetary resources. Absent more timely sources of earnings data and high-quality medical claim information to inform the determination process, this problem is likely to persist. In addition, the agency is further at risk due to its policies that allow claims examiners to unilaterally approve selected claims without independent supervisory review.

We recognize that ensuring the integrity of the T&P disability process presents a challenge for RRB. However, the lack of a robust quality assurance and continuous improvement framework has hindered RRB's ability to identify potential program integrity risks and aspects of the process that need to be improved. Absent comprehensive agency-wide performance goals and metrics to track and report on the accuracy of T&P determinations, RRB is also limited in its ability to monitor the extent to which the agency is making correct determinations and reduce its exposure to making improper payments. Finally, without clear policies and procedures for detecting, preventing, and addressing potentially fraudulent claims, RRB is unable to ensure the integrity of its process system-wide and that known program risks have been addressed. The weaknesses we identified in RRB's existing determination processes and policies require sustained management attention and a more proactive stance by the agency. Without such a commitment to fraud awareness and prevention, fraudulent claims may go undetected, and the agency risks undermining public confidence in its ability to administer the important programs under its jurisdiction.

Recommendations

To enhance RRB's ability to prevent improper payments and deter fraud in the T&P disability program, we recommend that the Railroad Retirement Board Members direct RRB staff to:

1. explore options to obtain more timely earnings data to ensure that claimants are working within allowable program limits prior to being awarded benefits;

2. revise the agency's policy concerning the supervisory review and approval of determinations to ensure that all T&P cases are reviewed by a second party;

3. strengthen oversight of the T&P determination process by establishing a regular quality assurance review of initial disability determinations to assess the quality of medical evidence, determination accuracy, and process areas in need of improvement;

4. develop performance goals to track the accuracy of disability determinations; and

5. develop procedures to identify and address cases of potential fraud before claims are approved, requiring annual training on these procedures for all agency personnel, and regularly communicating management's commitment to these procedures and to the principle that fraud awareness, identification, and prevention is the responsibility of all staff.

Agency Comments and Our Evaluation

We obtained written comments on a draft of this report from the Railroad Retirement Board. RRB agreed with all five of the recommendations we made to strengthen its management controls over the T&P disability determination process, and noted that it has already taken steps to implement the report's recommendations directed at improving the agency's ability to detect and deter fraud. RRB's formal comments are reproduced in appendix I. RRB also provided additional technical comments, which have been incorporated as appropriate.

As agreed with your offices, unless you publicly announce the contents of this report earlier, we plan no further distribution until 30 days from the report date. At that time, we will send copies to the Railroad Retirement Board, relevant congressional committees, and other interested parties. In addition, the report will be available at no charge on the GAO Web site at http://www.gao.gov.

If you or your staff have any questions about this report, please contact me at (202) 512-7215 or bertonid@gao.gov. Contact points for our Offices of Congressional Relations and Public Affairs may be found on the last page of this report. GAO staff who made key contributions to this report are listed in appendix II.

Sincerely yours,

Daniel Bertoni
Director, Education, Workforce,
 and Income Security Issues

Appendix I: Comments from the Railroad Retirement Board

UNITED STATES OF AMERICA
RAILROAD RETIREMENT BOARD
844 NORTH RUSH STREET
CHICAGO, ILLINOIS 60611-2092

BOARD MEMBERS:

MICHAEL S. SCHWARTZ, CHAIRMAN   June 6, 2014
WALTER A. BARROWS, LABOR MEMBER
STEVEN J. ANTHONY, MANAGEMENT MEMBER

Mr. Daniel Bertoni
Director
Education, Workforce, and Income Security Issues
United States Government Accountability Office
Washington, DC. 20548

Dear Mr. Bertoni,

Thank you for the opportunity to comment on your draft audit report Railroad Retirement
Board: Total and Permanent Disability Program at Risk of Improper Payments (GAO-14-418). Our
response to the the audit report, contents, findings, and recommendations follows. We have also
included technical comments as an attachment to our response.

Recommendation 1
Explore options to obtain more timely earnings data to ensure that claimants are working within
allowable program limits prior to being awarded benefits.

RRB Response
We agree. We will continue to explore opportunities to obtain more timely earnings data. Although
we have previously considered access to the National Directory of New Hires (NDNH), we will
resume our previously unsuccessful effort to obtain the required legislative authority to access
NDNH data as well as strategies for funding the initiative.

Recommendation 2
Revise the agency's policy concerning the supervisory review and approval of determinations to
ensure that all T&P cases are reviewed by a second party.

RRB Response
We agree. We will review our program practices to ensure that initial awards of the T&P disability
annuities are reviewed by a second party.

Recommendation 3
Strengthen oversight of the T&P determination process by establishing a regular quality assurance
review of initial disability determinations to assess the quality of medical evidence, determination
accuracy, and process areas in need of improvement.

 Printed on recycled paper

RRB Response

We agree. We will expand our quality assurance program to ensure that all critical activities of the disability initial determination process are addressed.

Recommendation 4

Develop performance goals to track the accuracy of disability determinations.

RRB Response

We agree. We will include the development of performance goals as part of our new quality assurance plan.

Recommendation 5

Develop procedures to identify and address cases of potential fraud before claims are approved, requiring annual training on these procedures for all agency personnel, and regularly communicating management's commitment to these procedures and to the principle that fraud awareness, identification, and prevention is the responsibility of all staff.

RRB Response

We agree. We are in the process of strengthening our pre-payment fraud detection effort which will include formal procedures and regular training to implement that procedure and that communicates the anti-fraud responsibilities of staff. We have convened a team of senior managers to guide our anti-fraud efforts. We are also considering contracting for an assessment of our existing fraud prevention and detection processes throughout our agency's operations by an independent source.

Sincerely,

Martha P. Rico
(FOR THE BOARD)
Secretary to the Board

Attachment: Technical Comments

Appendix II: GAO Contacts and Staff Acknowledgments

GAO Contact:	Daniel Bertoni, (202) 512-7215 or bertonid@gao.gov
Staff Acknowledgements	In addition to the contact named above, David Lehrer (Assistant Director), Arthur T. Merriam Jr. (Analyst-in-Charge), Carl Barden, Sue Bernstein, Jeremy Cox, Patrick Dibattista, Justin Dunleavy, Holly Dye, Alexander Galuten, Michael Kniss, Theresa Lo, Sheila McCoy, Jean McSween, Lorin Obler, Regina Santucci, Walter Vance made key contributions to this report.

Related GAO Products

Supplemental Security Income: SSA Has Taken Steps to Prevent and Detect Overpayments, but Additional Actions Could Be Taken to Improve Oversight. GAO-13-109. Washington, D.C.: December 14, 2012.

Disability Insurance: SSA Can Improve Efforts to Detect, Prevent, and Recover Overpayments. GAO-11-724. Washington, D.C.: July 27, 2011.

Use of the Railroad Retirement Board Occupational Disability Program across the Rail Industry. GAO-10-351R. Washington, D.C.: February 4, 2010.

Railroad Retirement Board: Review of Commuter Railroad Occupational Disability Claims Reveals Potential Program Vulnerabilities. GAO-09-821R. Washington, D.C.: September 9, 2009.

Railroad Retirement Board Disability Determinations. GAO/HRD-84-11. Washington, D.C.: July 20, 1984.